THE WOOD ENGRAVINGS OF
WILLIAM BLAKE

THE WOOD ENGRAVINGS OF
WILLIAM BLAKE

Seventeen subjects commissioned by
Dr Robert Thornton for his *Virgil* of 1821
newly printed from the original blocks
now in the British Museum

with an Introduction by
ANDREW WILTON
lately Assistant Keeper of Prints and Drawings

Published for the Trustees of the British Museum by
BRITISH MUSEUM PUBLICATIONS LTD
MCMLXXVII

150 sets of impressions from
Blake's original wood blocks
have been printed
of which 135 are for sale
numbered 1–135
15 out of series I–XV
This accompanying text published
February 1977

No. *118*

BM9 (BLA)

4988

ISBN 0 7141 0749 2

CONTENTS

KENNETH CLARK

Preface

Blake's pastoral woodcuts make their most magical effect in the form in which they first appeared, as illustrations in Thornton's *Pastorals of Virgil*, Vol. I. This is a mediocre piece of book production, badly printed and laid out, and the numerous wood blocks with which it is illustrated are of poor quality. Thornton gives a list of the illustrators and engravers employed, including Bewick, who certainly made no contribution himself, although some of his pupils may have done so; but the woodcuts are meagre and mechanical, and it remains a mystery how a man who produced one of the most beautiful English illustrated books of the early nineteenth century, *The Temple of Flora*, should have been responsible for such miserable volumes. Perhaps the answer he gives in his *Address to School-Masters and Parents* is sincere. He genuinely wanted to help children learn Latin by associating each line with a visual image; and he had in mind a small, useful school book published at a fairly modest price. In order to encourage his young readers he also included an English poem, an imitation of Virgil's *First Eclogue* by Ambrose Philips, and it is this that he invited Blake to illustrate. The results were so stunningly different from all his other illustrations, that he felt bound to preface them with a note 'The Illustrations of this English Pastoral are by the famous B L A K E, the illustrator of *Young's* Night Thoughts, and *Blair's* Grave; who designed and engraved them himself. This is mentioned, as they display less of art than genius, and are much admired by some eminent painters.' This apologia is usually quoted as an expression of disappointment, or even malice, but I do not read it in this sense. Any ordinary teacher or young person turning over the pages of Thornton's book, would surely have been much surprised when he came to the illustrations by Blake, and would have felt the need of some explanation. If by 'art' is meant the clear, informative use of the mediums that Bewick had brought to perfection, then Blake's cuts do indeed 'show less of art than genius'.

I will not say that Blake was inspired by Ambrose Philips's poem (although it is not without charm), but it certainly released in Blake a feeling for pastoral poetry and for landscape in general, which might otherwise have been confined to very few works such as the backgrounds of *Job*. He has not tried to vary Thornton's formula, that is to say, he has put four cuts together on a page, each of them illustrating a stanza or even a line in the text opposite. In most cases he has done so quite literally, so that the line 'a rolling stone is ever bare of moss' is illustrated by the image of a boy pulling a stone lawn-roller. The weakest work in the series is a conscientious attempt to illustrate the line 'for him our yearly wakes and feasts we hold', which is outside the pastoral spirit of the rest. But when a link, or even a word – 'ill fated tree' – gives him a chance to extend his imagination, he produced those marvels of poetic analogy which, as Thornton says, 'have been much admired by some eminent painters', from their first appearance to our own day, from Samuel Palmer to Graham Sutherland.

I need add nothing to what has been written about the beauty of Blake's woodcuts. A glowing imagination is compressed into these images, so that the longer one looks at them the more poetic inventions one discovers. In these small works, done in humble acceptance of a publisher's demands, there is a quality of lyric poetry greater than in any of the illustrations to Blake's own *Songs of Innocence and Experience*. We are left marvelling at the unpredictable nature of inspiration.

IAIN BAIN AND DAVID CHAMBERS

The Printing of the Blocks
A Technical Note

In 1937, when the Nonesuch Press published Sir Geoffrey Keyne's account of his rediscovery of Blake's blocks for Thornton's *Virgil*, the blocks were used to make electrotypes from which impressions were taken to accompany the essay. This was quite the best way to produce accurate reproductions for a substantial edition. The result was an impressive improvement on the original printing in the book of 1821, and the random prints taken off by Linnell in later years. But recent inspection of the blocks showed us that there was still a certain amount of detail in some of them that the electrotype printing had failed to pick up, but which could be brought out with careful work direct from the wood.

It was our possession and regular printing of original blocks engraved on the end-grain of boxwood by Thomas Bewick that first prompted us to look at Blake's work in the same medium. Bewick's blocks, cut at the end of the eighteenth century, print as well today as when first produced, and this remarkable resilience of the boxwood gave us confidence that the *Virgil* engravings would print equally successfully and without risk of wear.

Blake set out by engraving four subjects at a time on a single unusually large piece of box—he may well have found this easier to handle than small pieces the size of a single subject. By reassembling the blocks in their original close grouping, our detailed examination showed that the surface had not been particularly well prepared before he started work. Some curious curved depressions running across the blocks are very evident and seem to be the result of an inadequate scraping-finish and polishing. It may be that Blake cut his own blocks direct from the log of boxwood, as Bewick did, and being perhaps a newcomer to practical wood engraving was not fully competent in the processing of the raw wood. One of the blocks, No. 9, also has some

[9]

surface damage that plainly occurred at the time of the first printing: there is a bad scratch down the right-hand side which looks as if it might have been a miscalculated saw-mark, and the outline of a large pin or nail runs diagonally across the block—it must be assumed that something of the sort was inadvertently left on the surface before an impression was taken. These blemishes can be seen in the reproductions of the light impressions which we took on a hard baryta paper (Plate 2).

The overlays which we prepared for printing in the traditional nineteenth-century fashion, for the increase of pressure on the full black areas, were also elaborated to carry the paper into the surface blemishes. The nature of some of them can be seen in Plate 3. It was also necessary to prepare underlays for many of the blocks to compensate for their uneven height. This further irregularity in the finish of the blocks gives weight to the supposition that Blake prepared his own material, for by this time it would have been possible to buy prepared box or else the proper equipment for the process. (Bewick's blocks for his *Fables* of 1818 are very truly squared and well finished, in great contrast to his blocks of the 1790s.) Blake's frontispiece block, the largest in the series, is the one exception, and it looks as if it might have been bought fully prepared.

The basic condition of the blocks is perfectly sound, and indeed they are completely free of the knot-holes and cracks frequently to be found in the edges and undersides of Bewick's earlier engravings. Nevertheless, it was obviously essential to take every precaution against possible damage from any accidentally heavy printing pressure. We therefore devised and built up a forme that accommodated two blocks at a time, with a full surround to each of $1\frac{1}{2}$ inch wide type-high (i.e. block-high) bearers of sycamore.

The press brought to the Museum premises for the work was David Chambers's 12 × 20 inch Alexandra, built in 1884—an iron hand-press constructed on the original Albion principle. As we wanted to avoid all possibility of the 'picking' of paper fibres from the image as each print was removed from the printing surface, we decided against using the conventional frisket—the metal frame which holds the paper to the tympan of the press while an impression is taken. In its place two alternatives of manilla card were hinged into each end of the forme. These enabled us to place the paper directly to the block, and, most importantly, allowed us to peel off each print slowly and care-

1. Two blocks in the press, locked up for printing; the hinged friskets can be seen raised at each end of the forme. *Photo H. Warhurst*

2. Three impressions on baryta paper, before make-ready and showing surface indentation.

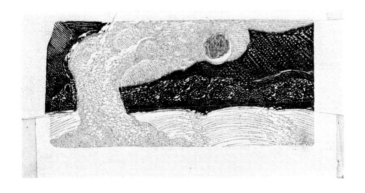

3. Make-ready for three of the blocks, showing areas of built up tissue overlays for local increase of pressure in printing. The upper two show the edges of the overlays teased out; the overlays for the third block have hard edges and, for accuracy, have been cut out from a print.

4. The printers, Iain Bain (top) and David Chambers,
taking off impressions. *Photos H. Warhurst*

fully after its impression—to minimise the pull of the very stiff ink on the paper's surface. The use of manilla card also enabled us to avoid any risk of the damage to the blocks that might have come from the accidental contact of a metal frisket had we used one.

As much of Blake's cutting is very fine and shallow—a clear indication of his metal-engraving background—the press's tympan had to be hard-packed with cartridge paper, and the surface of the tympan carried the specially built up overlays of tissue and blotting paper to secure the local adjustment and gradation of printing pressures already referred to.

The ink used was a 'stiff lithographic' proofing black supplied by T. N. Lawrence & Son and it was applied with small 2-inch and 4-inch plastic hand-rollers—which sometimes had to be tilted to reach lowered edges and corners. (Normally block-high bearers would be positioned at the edge of the forme to provide a driving surface for the roller.) For each impression the blocks were rolled two or three times with a very fine film of ink.

The best paper available was a calendered Japanese Hosho, also supplied by T. N. Lawrence & Son, which prints extremely well without having to be damped. A good many impressions were rejected during the course of printing: it was difficult to keep the ink film at just the right point to give a full richness of result without clogging the very finely engraved areas; nor could we use a heavier impression with a lighter film—so much of the cutting is extremely shallow. Thus the rate of printing achieved as low a figure as 30 copies per hour. But the results have been rewarding and demonstrate most clearly that impressions taken in the nineteenth century did little justice to the beauty of the blocks, and that hand printing from the original wood has in several respects improved on the excellent machine printing from electrotypes of the 1930s.

ANDREW WILTON

Blake's Illustrations for
Thornton's Virgil

The British Museum acquired Blake's seventeen woodblocks for Dr
Thornton's Virgil primer in 1939;[1] they were presented by the
National Art-Collections Fund, which purchased them at a sale of
some property of John Linnell in December 1938,[2] and at the same
time gave the Museum Blake's only other work on wood, the uncut
design of *Isaiah foretelling the Destruction of Jerusalem*, from the same
source.[3] Linnell had bought the Virgil blocks while Blake was still
alive, from Thornton's agent, W. Harrison, a wine merchant of 13,
Little Tower Street, in the City. Thornton signed a receipt for the
transaction on September 16, 1825, which ran: 'Received of Mr
Linnell for the Wood-Blocks executed by Mr Blake two guineas for
Mr Mr Mr [*sic*] Harrison'.[4]

While they were in his possession, Linnell took a number of impressions from the blocks, some on india paper; these are the only sets to
exist outside the book for which they were intended, though some
proofs pulled by Blake himself do survive,[5] and odd subjects were
later printed for particular purposes: No. 3, for instance, was published in *The Athenaeum* for January 21, 1843, as a comparison with
the recutting of the same design by a hack; and blocks 5, 6 and 9
illustrate Gilchrist's *Life of Blake*.[6] Although they have been repro-

---

[1] Registered as nos. 1939–14–1–2 to 18.

[2] Christie's, 2nd December 1938, lot 60. Lots 60 to 63 were 'Sold by Order of the Surviving
Trustee of the late John Linnell, Esq., Senior'. They had been found among the effects of Herbert
Linnell, a trustee of the Linnell estate which included much Blake material. See Geoffrey
Keynes, 'The Blake-Linnell Documents', and 'Thornton's Virgil', in *Blake Studies*, 1949, pp.
135 ff., and 157 ff.

[3] B.M. no. 1939–14–1–19. Repr. Keynes, *Blake Studies*, pl. 37.

[4] Transcribed in A. H. Palmer, *Catalogue of an Exhibition of Drawings, Etchings & Woodcuts by
Samuel Palmer and other Disciples of William Blake*, Victoria and Albert Museum, 1926, no. 28,
p. 28.

[5] See note 22 below.

[6] Alexander Gilchrist, *Life of William Blake*, 2nd ed., 1880, vol. I, facing p. 320.

duced on various occasions since 1899,[7] notably from the electrotypes made for the Nonesuch edition of 1937,[8] there has hitherto been no modern reprint directly from the woodblocks themselves, which are still in excellent condition.[9]

The beauty and originality of the illustrations that Blake made for Thornton contrast so surprisingly—so shockingly—with the dull work among which they were published that our instinctive reaction is to transfer our own sense of shock to Blake himself: how could such a genius tolerate the ignominy of working for such a publisher and such a publication?[10] Only the material failure of Blake's career, which obliged him to accept unrewarding hack commissions, could have prompted him to undertake a project so alien to him. That Thornton was a man to whom Blake was naturally hostile can be demonstrated both by his reception of Blake's work and by Blake's attack on the Translation of the Lord's Prayer that Thornton published in 1827.[11] It is the miracle of Blake's genius, we conclude, which is alone responsible for the grandeur and poetry that he wrested from wholly unpromising, not to say stultifying material.

It was Blake's young admirer, John Linnell,[12] who was responsible for his introduction to the Linnell family physician, Robert John Thornton, M.D.[13] and, no doubt, for the suggestion that Thornton might commission the artist to contribute to his Virgil project. The 'School Virgil' had been in print since 1812,[14] and Thornton had early on conceived the idea of using illustrations to make learning easier. He had advertised the 'Price of this Volume, bound, with only a few Cuts, Eight Shillings—with numerous Wood-Cuts, (most of the Ideas

---

[7] The woodcuts were first reproduced in an edition of '450 copies, royal octavo, printed on Van Gelder hand-made paper' by Thomas B. Mosher, of 45 Exchange Street, Portland, Maine, 1899. Mosher issued J. W. Mackail's translation of Virgil's *Eclogues* and *Georgics* in the same year, illustrated with some of Samuel Palmer's Virgil etchings.

[8] *The Illustrations of William Blake for Thornton's Virgil with the First Eclogue and the Imitation by Ambrose Philips*, introduced by Geoffrey Keynes, Nonesuch Press, 1937. Keynes's Introduction was reprinted with emendations in *Blake Studies*; see note 2 above.

[9] See the note by Iain Bain and David Chambers on the printing of the new edition, in this volume, p. 9.

[10] Its title-page reads: 'The Pastorals of Virgil, with a course of English Reading, adapted for Schools: in which all the proper facilities are given, enabling youth to acquire the Latin Language, in the shortest period of time. Illustrated by 230 Engravings. By Robert John Thornton, M.D. Member of the University of Cambridge, &c.&c. Third Edition . . . London: Stereotyped and Printed by J. M'Gowan, Great Windmill Street . . . 1821. N.B. The Price of Thornton's Pastorals of Virgil, is 15s. bound. A full Allowance to the Trade and Schoolmasters.'

[11] See below, note 25.

[12] John Linnell, 1792–1882.

[13] Thornton's date of birth is not known for certain; it was probably 1768. He died in 1837.

[14] Entitled, in full: 'School Virgil: whereby Boys will acquire Ideas as well as Words; Masters be saved the necessity of any explanation; and the Latin Language obtained in the shortest time.'

of Virgil being Pictured) Twelve Shillings'; and in 1814 a slim volume was issued separately with a set of illustrations.[15] A second edition of the primer appeared in 1819, and the third was planned to incorporate illustrations on an exceptionally lavish scale. The preliminary 'Address to School-Masters and Parents' in the new edition propounds a theory of 'audio-visual' instruction that anticipates modern attitudes to language teaching:

'Why is it, that a *child* so soon acquires its *native* language? Because to each *word* with them, a correspondent *idea* is attached; and when once *boys* begin to *think*, instead of learning *words* by rote, as *parrots*, it is inconceivable the rapid progress they afterwards make in knowledge . . .'

Thornton's progressive approach to teaching Latin was typical of his enthusiastic, and limitedly creative, intelligence, which showed itself especially in his interest in Botany; this had resulted in several publications and had brought into existence one of the most sumptuous collections of botanical illustrations ever produced: the *Temple of Flora*, to which Thornton even contributed one subject painted by himself. It was printed in fine type and liberally strewn with poetical quotations, and was, as Thornton himself admitted, an attempt to produce in the realm of science what Boydell's *Shakspeare* and *Milton* had done for the national literature: in imitation of the Shakspeare Gallery, he even held an exhibition of the botanical paintings which were the basis of the book.[16]

Thornton had, then, an active interest in art, and had given some thought to the role of illustration, recognising the value that suitable visual stimuli might have for students. He therefore proposed that his elaborately explanatory *Virgil*, with its Imitations by other poets, notes and assorted aids to learning, should be enhanced by a comprehensive system of illustrations, giving schoolboys a visual image

[15] 'Illustrations of the School-Virgil, in Copper-plates, and Wood-cuts; whereby Boys will learn with greater facility; deeper impressions be made; and ideas acquired, at the same time, as words.'

[16] See *An Account of Dr. Thornton's Exhibition of Botanical Paintings; now open at No 49, New Bond Street; with the Poetic Compositions made on the different Subjects, and Explanatory Notes*, London, 1804. Thornton's principal botanical works are: *Practical Botany*, 1808; *Botanical Extracts, or Philosophy of Botany*, 1810; *Elementary Botanical Plates to Illustrate 'Botanical Extracts'*, 1810 (165 plates); *Alpha Botanica*, 1810; *A New Family Herbal*, 1810 (with woodcuts attributed to Bewick but cut by his apprentices after drawings by Henderson); *A Grammar of Botany*, 1811; *The British Flora*, 1812. The *Temple of Flora* appeared in parts between 1798 and 1807, in which year it was published in Thornton's *New Illustration of the Sexual System of Carolus von Linnaeus . . . and the Temple of Flora, or Garden of Nature*, with a fulsome dedication to the Queen. A second edition appeared in 1812. It included 31 of an intended 70 plates. Thornton's own contribution was *Roses* engraved by Earlom, 1805. It is inferior to the others. See Geoffrey Grigson and Handasyde Buchanan, *Thornton's Temple of Flora*, 1951.

for every verbal one. These illustrations were to be arranged on the page as far as possible so that they fell exactly opposite the relevant text; hence the format of the small octavo volume was very cramped, and each block had to be very small. The conscientious Doctor, genuinely anxious to do well by students, teachers and artists alike, hoped to enlist the aid of the most competent professionals that could be found. He claimed that 'in order to render this work worthy, as much as possible, of public patronage, and the distinguished honour conferred on it, by the approbation of the learned, Messrs. *Thurston, Craig, Cruickshanks [sic], Blake* and *Varley*,[17] with others of great merit, have been selected for the designs; while the most eminent engravers on wood have been employed, as *Nesbit, Clennell, Branston, Bewick, Thomson, Hughes, Byfield, Williams, Lee, Mackenzie,* and *Sears*,[18] for the *Cuts*, so that Boys will now learn Latin with *greater facility* and *pleasure* to themselves, *deeper impressions* be made, and *ideas*, as well as *words*, be acquired.' All these names were, indeed, 'eminent', and Thornton was no doubt unaware how far his claims were in excess of the facts: it does not appear that Bewick himself actually touched any of the blocks of the *Virgil*—he had indeed retired from general trade work by 1812; but his pupils may have engraved a few subjects, and no deception was intended. Thornton will have embraced John Linnell's recommendation of his friend Blake with gratitude, pleased to help an artist in need, and expecting the best. The commission was put in hand in 1820. No doubt he was satisfied with the six purely factual plates engraved by Blake in plain outline on copper, showing the heads of Theocritus, Virgil, Augustus, Agrippa, Julius Caesar and Epicurus, taken from busts and coins;[19] and with the drawing that Blake made of Poussin's *Landscape with*

[17] Thornton's designers were: John Thurston, 1744–1822; William Marshall Craig, fl. 1788–1829; probably Isaac Robert Cruikshank (rather than George), 1789–1856; Blake, 1757–1827; and John Varley, 1778–1842.

[18] The engravers cited by Thornton were: Charlton Nesbit, 1775–1838; Luke Clennell, 1781–1840; Allen Robert Branston, 1778–1827; Thomas Bewick, 1753–1828; and, probably, John Thompson, 1785–1866. The other names in Thornton's list are less easy to identify; 'Williams' may be Samuel Williams, 1788–1853; 'Hughes' is perhaps William Hughes, d.1825; 'Lee' James Lee; and 'Sears' M. U. Sears; 'Mackenzie' is possibly the engraver of that name entered in Thieme-Becker as working about 1800. Nesbit and Clennell had been apprentices of Bewick and the book shows almost no evidence of their hands; Thompson had been taught by Branston who came from a Norfolk metal-engraving workshop, and though they and the other men named flourished on the impetus provided by Bewick, they were to develop a quite separate intricate 'black-line' school of reproductive engraving. But for the most part they should have been capable of work of a higher order than that seen in the *Virgil*, so it may be that Thornton was unable to raise sufficient funds to pay for superior results.

[19] A. G. B. Russell, *The Engravings of William Blake*, 1912, 30, xxii–xxvii.

Polyphemus, which Byfield cut to illustrate Eclogue II.[20] But his distress and disappointment at being so sadly incapable of following Blake's highly individual path in the illustrations to Ambrose Philips's Imitation of the First Eclogue can be read between the lines of the apology that he had printed under the frontispiece:

'The Illustrations of this English Pastoral are by the famous BLAKE, illustrator of *Young's* Night Thoughts, and *Blair's* Grave; who designed and engraved them himself. This is mentioned, as they display less of art than genius, and are much admired by some eminent painters.'

They had been admired, in fact, by no less an authority than the President of the Royal Academy, Sir Thomas Lawrence, as well as by James Ward and others, including, of course, Linnell. Thornton had met these men at the dinner-table of the German collector Charles Aders;[21] their opinion cannot but have impressed him, and their judgement of Blake's woodcuts compelled him, conscientious as he was, to reconsider his decision to scrap the blocks and have the designs recut by a 'professional'. He did so with a sense of his own inadequacy, which however he defended in his note: it is, in a way, more of a self-confession than a criticism of Blake.

Even so, three of Blake's designs were sacrificed at the hands of a commercial engraver—the three illustrating the 'comparisons' in the penultimate speech of the Imitation—and all the rest were cut down to fit the crowded pages of the primer, a contingency that Blake seems to have tried to avoid, judging from the way he printed his early proofs, with four designs on a single uncut block so that they are packed tightly together on each sheet.[22] Even so, it seems likely that

---

[20] Facing page 21 (with a misprinted reference to Eclogue I); Russell, 30, xxi. The picture by Poussin is in the Hermitage, Leningrad (Anthony Blunt, *The Paintings of Nicolas Poussin,* 1966, cat. no. 169, pl. 190).

[21] Gilchrist, *Life,* vol. I, p. 318. For Aders, see Mona Wilson, *The Life of William Blake,* revised edition, 1948, p. 286.

[22] Proofs of some of the blocks (nos. 2–9), printed before trimming, are extant two: sheets, with four blocks to a sheet, are in the British Museum Print Room, presented by Herbert Linnell, 1919–5–28–2 and 3; another impression of the first sheet was in the collection of Frank Rinder, and impressions of the second are in the collections of Philip Hofer and the Fitzwilliam Museum, Cambridge. These proof impressions measure about 4 by 8.8 cm. The trimmed blocks measure approx. 3.5 by 7.5 cm., having lost between 5 and 10 mm. by about 10 mm. The larger frontispiece measures 6.2 by 8.4 cm.; being alone on the page it was not cut down. It has been argued (e.g. by Laurence Binyon, 'Blake's Woodcuts', *Burlington Magazine,* VII, December 1920, pp. 284–9) that the proofs from the untrimmed blocks indicate that further work was done on them by hands other than Blake's before the printing of the edition. This does not seem to be necessarily the case: the proofs differ by reason of variations in inking and paper; such alterations as there are (the change in the skyline in block 9, for instance) were probably Blake's own modifications. Keynes (*Blake Studies,* p. 160) suggests that the intensity of the woodcuts is enhanced

he accepted the terms of the commission in a spirit of professional realism, and himself trimmed the blocks when it became clear that they were too large. He can hardly have spurned Thornton for compelling him to make these changes as tradition romantically suggests: in 1825 he engraved a small plate of *The Hiding of the Infant Moses in the Bulrushes* for a pocket Annual, *Remember Me!* that Thornton published. Keynes surmises[23] that this was done at Linnell's instigation again; Linnell would not have suggested such a thing if Blake and Thornton were already at daggers drawn, and it must be supposed that the *Virgil* affair passed off without too much ill-feeling. Indeed, there is evidence that Blake was to have made a further plate for another issue of Thornton's annual.[24] When he attacked Thornton it was two years later still, and over the specific subject of Thornton's translation of the Lord's Prayer, which contained very definite points of conflict with Blake's philosophy, by this date unequivocally polarised in antagonism to 'The Greek and Roman Classics . . . the Antichrist', and to 'Newtonian & Baconian' materialism.[25] Obviously, his experience of the Doctor's approach to art will have coloured his view of Thornton's fitness as a religious commentator. The *Virgil* had already provided Thornton with the excuse (in the 'prophecies' of the fourth Eclogue) for a very extensive religious discussion; Blake took the opportunity supplied by Thornton's 'Tory Translation, Translated out of its disguise in the Classical & Scotch languages' (alluding to Thornton's Scottish descent) to scribble on the flyleaf his own diatribe: 'Thus we see that the Real God is the Goddess Nature, and that God creates nothing but what can be Touch'd & Weighed & Taxed & Measured; all else is Heresy & Rebellion against Caesar, Virgil's only God—see Eclogue I; for all this we thank Dr Thornton.'

It is true, then, that Blake may have felt a profound hostility towards Thornton's *Virgil* in so far as it represented a system of education that uncritically admired the classical cultures which he had come to despise; it was Thornton's conservative, classically-oriented temperament that was offensive—that he would misunderstand Blake's astringent art might go without saying. And yet the

---

by their being crowded together. There is certainly every reason to believe that Blake took the stipulated format of the book into account when designing his blocks, and that he himself was responsible for the cutting-down necessary to make them fit Thornton's book. See plates 5 and 6.

[23] *Blake Studies*, pp. 186–190 and pl. 47.
[24] *Blake Studies*, p. 190.
[25] Blake, *Complete Writings*, ed. Geoffrey Keynes, corrected paperback edition, 1971, pp. 786–9.

Two engravings by another hand from elsewhere in the
Virgil, shown for comparison with Blake's treatment of
similar subject matter. See p. 19 and n. 26.

very nature of Blake's success in the *Virgil* commission is evidence
enough that he found the work congenial—satisfying on a level that
touched the core of his creative personality. In spite of the theoretical
context, the immediate matter was unexceptionable. A comparison of
one or two of his designs with examples by other illustrators taken
from elsewhere in the *Virgil*[26] shows that Blake did not depart from
the subject-matter that was dictated: his themes are similar to theirs;
all that is different is the treatment, and that differs not in being *less*
fully engaged, but in being *more* so. Blake was, in fact, deeply and
consciously sympathetic to the task he had undertaken.

Perhaps it is surprising, nonetheless, that so insignificant a poem as
Ambrose Philips's Pastoral in Imitation of Virgil's First Eclogue should
have been inspiration for a man in the habit of turning to Milton,
Dante and the Bible for his themes. But Blake was thoroughly im-
mersed in the eighteenth-century poetic tradition; some of his most
extensive exercises as an illustrator were in connection with the work
of Gray, Young and Blair—men whom we now regard as archetypes
of their literary period, and without whose example Blake's own
Prophetic Books could not have been formed as they are. His lyrical
poems, too, have direct links with the immediate past. The reliance of
the *Songs of Innocence* and *Experience* on Isaac Watts's devotional
poems and hymns has been pointed out,[27] and they are equally clearly
connected with the Augustan tradition of Pastoral. Shenstone's

> My banks they are furnished with bees,
>   Whose murmur invites one to sleep;
> My grottoes are shaded with trees,
>   And my hills are white over with sheep[28]

is an example of the fusion of the Virgilian Arcadia with the landscape
of the Psalms that crystallised in the late seventeenth century and

---

[26] E.g. the block illustrating lines 66–8 of Eclogue II, facing p. 26, which shows a yoke of oxen at
sunset; and the frontispiece to Eclogue III, facing p. 40, *Corydon and Battus*, which is almost
identical in subject to Blake's frontispiece. See opposite.

[27] By S. Foster Damon, *William Blake: His Philosophy and Symbols*, 1924, p. 41.

[28] William Shenstone (1714–63), *A Pastoral Ballad*, in four parts, 1743, part II, 'Hope', lines 1–4.
Damon (loc. cit.) denies that the *Songs of Innocence* belong to any tradition: 'Watts is the only
author we can positively name whose writings may have affected these *Songs* even slightly.'
Blake's originality in these lyrics is abundantly evident, but they can nevertheless be said to
derive some of their literary characteristics from existing models. The *Poetical Sketches* (*Writings*,
pp. 1 ff.) include examples, such as the *Song* (p. 10), that imitate conventional Pastoral forms.
This is not to contradict F. R. Leavis's assertion that Blake 'represents the antithesis to the
Augustan ethos' (*Revaluation*, 1936, p. 122), and Blake's philosophical content is, of course,
wholly his own. Other influences on the early Blake, especially Spenser and Milton, are discussed
in Michael Phillips, 'Blake's Early Poetry' in *Essays in honour of Sir Geoffrey Keynes*, ed. Morton
D. Paley and Michael Phillips, 1973, pp. 1–28.

which has a direct bearing on Blake's own evocations of landscape, both in late works like the Thornton illustrations, and in early ones such as the *Songs of Innocence*:

> How sweet is the shepherd's sweet lot
> From the morn to the evening he strays;
> He shall follow his sheep all the day
> And his mouth shall be filled with praise.

The page on which this poem, *The Shepherd*, occurs (f.5 of the *Songs of Innocence*) is decorated with a landscape in which a shepherd stands under a tree contemplating his flock. The image is recurrent in the *Songs of Innocence*—there are echoes of it in the frontispiece, in the plate of *The Lamb* (f.8), *The Little Black Boy* (f.10—where the shepherd is Christ) and *Spring* (f.22); and it appears in the frontispiece to the *Songs of Experience*, though not, significantly, elsewhere among those poems. It is an image identical with that of the opening lines of Philips' Pastoral:

> Is it not Colinet I lonesome see,
> leaning with folded arms against the tree?—

Blake's woodcut illustrating these words uses elements that he had already appropriated for his first important book of poems. The simplicity, the naivety of Philips's verse was not out of sympathy with that of Blake's own. And its essential matter, using the rustic life as the type of human happiness, was a central theme of Blake's: the antithesis of 'England's pleasant pastures green' and 'those dark Satanic mills'[29] is a development of it. There are other, more particular parallels. Philips's 'Moon, by wizard charm'd' that 'foreshows, Blood-stain'd in foul eclipse, impending woes' is a vivid visual image not unlike one in Blake's *The Mental Traveller*:

> The stars, sun, Moon, all shrink away,
> A desart vast without a bound,
> And nothing left to eat or drink,
> And a dark desart all around.[30]

Again, the 'naked tree/ Which bears the thunder-scar . . . The mark of storms, and sport of every wind' is a darker presentation of the symbol of himself that Blake had delightedly opened on by chance in Dryden's translation of Virgil:

[29] From the Preface to *Milton*, 1804; *Writings*, pp. 480–1.

[30] *Writings*, pp. 424–7. This strange poem is elucidated by Kathleen Raine, *Blake and Tradition*, 1968, vol. I, chap. XIII, pp. 306 ff. See also Harold Fisch, 'Blake's Miltonic Armour' in *Essays for S. Foster Damon*, 1969, p. 43.

As, when the winds their airy quarrel try,
Justling from every quarter of the sky;
This way and that the mountain oak they bend
His boughs they shatter and his branches rend . . .
Unmov'd the royal plant their fury mocks,
Or shaken clings more closely to the rocks,
For as he shoots his towering head on high
So deep in earth his fix'd foundations lie.[31]

And Colinet's complaint:

Untoward lads, the wanton imps of spite
make mock of all the ditties I indite.—

must also have recommended itself as peculiarly relevant to Blake,
who was perhaps able to realise Philips's Menalcas (parallel to Augustus
in Virgil's Eclogue) not as a false god[32] but rather as the benevolent
patron of the arts that the poet certainly intended him to be, having
his own patron Addison in mind:

he, good to all who good deserves, shall give
thy flock to feed, and thee at ease to live,
shall curb the malice of unbridled tongues,
and bounteously reward thy rural songs.—

These are all local details of imagery and sentiment which may have
contributed to Blake's sense of engagement with the poem. There is
another which offers a more significant insight into his view of the
world of Pastoral: the Imitation ends with a picture of 'the signs of
ebbing day' which might be seen as setting the stage for Gray's *Elegy
in a Country Churchyard*:

'With songs the jovial hinds return from plow,
And unyok'd heifers, loitering homeward, low.'

Blake seizes on the reference to the plough and includes one in both of
his final designs for the series of woodcuts. It was for him a symbol
perhaps even more personal than the shepherd with his flock. The
only occasion on which he incorporated his own portrait into one of
his works was when he used himself as the model for the Plowman in

---

[31] From Dryden's translation of the *Aeneid*, book IV, lines 638–647. Blake transcribed the lines in
1807; *Writings*, pp. 440–1. They are printed with some differences: 'bear' and 'tear' for 'bend'
and 'rend' in lines 640 and 641, and 'lowring' for towering' in line 646.

[32] In the first Eclogue Virgil refers to Caesar Augustus allegorically as a god:
'O Melibœe, deus nobis haec otia fecit:
namque, erit ille mihi semper deus';
Thornton comments on this as 'a species of flattery of a degrading nature, but suited to the
times.' Compare Philips's tribute to Addison as 'Menalcas' in his Imitation, lines 112–128.

his picture of the *Canterbury Pilgrims*, and the engraving he made from it.[33] It is likely that the profile self-portrait that appears in the Rossetti notebook[34] was used as the basis for the likeness, as it corresponds in almost every feature, except in the thinness of the Plowman's throat, a difference that is explained by Blake in his description of the picture:

> 'The Plowman is simplicity itself, with wisdom and strength for its stamina. Chaucer has divided the ancient character of Hercules between his Miller and his Plowman. Benevolence is the Plowman's great characteristic; he is thin with excessive labour, and not with old age, as some have supposed:
>
> > He would thresh, and thereto dike and delve
> > For Christe's sake, for every poore wight,
> > Withouten hire, if it lay in his might.
>
> . . . The Plowman of Chaucer is Hercules in his eternal state, divested of his spectrous shadow, which is the Miller . . .'[35]

Blake saw the ploughman, then, as a figure of real seriousness, not merely as a decorative or sentimental adjunct to rusticity. It is perhaps worth noting in this connection the little symbolic anecdote that he recounted after his arrival at Felpham in 1800:

> 'I met a plow on my first going out at my gate the first morning after my arrival, & the Plowboy said to the Plowman, "Father, The Gate is Open."'[36]

Blake not only saw and expressed much of what he felt about the world in terms of strongly felt pastoral imagery: he identified himself with a very specific pastoral type; hence, we may surmise, his repetition of the 'signature' motif of the plough at the end of the set of woodcuts.

Johnson, who pronounced that Philips 'has added nothing to English poetry', admitted that 'at least half his book deserves to be read',[37] and included in that half the Pastorals and lyrics (even if he did not attach much weight to the heptasyllabic couplets that earned Philips the nickname of 'Namby Pamby'—his most enduring contribution to the language). Blake's intensity could find value in the

[33] The 'fresco' is in the Pollock House collection, Glasgow. The engraving is catalogued in Keynes, *Engravings by William Blake, The Separate Plates*, 1956, no. XVII, pls. 27–33.

[34] British Library, Add. MS. 49460, f. 67. See Keynes, 'Blake's Notebook', *Blake Studies*, pp. 13–20 and pl. 7.

[35] *Writings*, p. 571.

[36] *Writings*, p. 803.

[37] Samuel Johnson, *Lives of the English Poets*, Everyman Edition, 1954, vol. II, p. 307.

threadbare covering that Philips gave an ancient theme which was of a relevance both personal and universal. He was embarking on a restatement of the motifs of Innocence in the light of thirty years' bitter experience.

There was therefore an ironic significance in the new medium of wood-engraving into which Blake sallied for the work. It demanded a verve and spontaneity that stripped the familiar subjects of their sweetness, investing them with a pungency entirely apt to the sharper mood of Blake's late years. It has been noticed[38] that there was in fact nothing essentially new in the experiment—except the wood itself: the 'white line' technique that is so striking in the woodcuts had appeared frequently in Blake's work, and occurs even as early as the late 1780s in the etching of *The Approach of Doom*[39] that he made after a drawing by his brother Robert and printed in relief—i.e., with ink on the surface of the plate rather than in the etched lines. Many of the 'stereotype' plates, from which the illuminated books were printed, embody something of the ambiguity of the relief print in which light becomes darkness, foreground becomes background: sometimes, as in the full-page illustrations to *Milton* and *Jerusalem*, the decorative and emotional intention of the design is achieved by printing the plate in black, so that forms appear as if illuminated by a brilliant white light. A small plate, *The Man sweeping the Interpreter's Parlour*,[40] engraved on pewter and unrelated to any of the books, has not only the intermittent, silvery lighting that is characteristic of the *Virgil* woodcuts but even a compositional layout common in them: two figures at either side of a rather elongated horizontal scene, as we find in the first four *Virgil* illustrations.

Blake was, indeed, perfectly well equipped to tackle wood, as he had handled copper and pewter before. The first block, the frontispiece to the Pastoral, which is larger than the others, is executed in a manner that shows how completely a professional he was. The figures are modelled with parallel lines of great precision, the subtle turn of a limb or muscle implied with classic control of the graver. In the less specific parts of the design—the landscape lit by the rising sun— Blake's touch is broken into allusive, flickering strokes that do not partake of conventional linear explicitness. It is precisely in these

[38] By Laurence Binyon, 'The Engravings of William Blake and Edward Calvert', *Print Collectors' Quarterly*, vol. VII, 1917, pp. 307–332; and by Keynes, *Blake Studies*, p. 159.
[39] *The Separate Plates*, no. IV, pl. 8.
[40] *The Separate Plates*, no. VII, pls. 18, 19.

areas that the mystical world of the woodcuts is fully realised; and in the remaining, smaller blocks that delicate, rapid, evanescent touch is universal. The neat parallels in the figures and sky of the frontispiece become liquid, blending together, blurring and shifting over the forms, like moonlight, as Laurence Binyon has observed.[41] Even so the firm foundation of vigorous draughtsmanship is there; the movement and musculature of the man rolling the path in block 10, for example, are very fully and accurately rendered; and in the same block the weight of the roller itself is expressed by a quite academic use of parallel cuts.

Blake's style as an engraver on wood, then, was one that he adopted deliberately, with particular results in mind. At the very outset he consciously remodelled his highly disciplined and experienced technique, not so much to a new medium as to a new mood. And when he returned to copper, in the *Job* engravings of 1823–6, his approach was evidently modified by what amounts to the technical liberation that he had experienced in working on wood. The pastoral landscape of *Thus did Job continually*,[42] and several others of the set, is handled in a roughly stippled manner that seems to derive directly from the flecked technique of the woodcuts.[43]

One of the most remarkable tokens of his independence is the total absence of influence from the established master of the woodcut vignette, Thomas Bewick. Bewick's workshop executed other illustrations for Thornton,[44] and it is his manner that influences all the other cuts in the primer which attempt the 'white-line' method, albeit for the most part abysmally debased. Such a wide-ranging and experimental technique as Bewick's was likely to embrace idioms that might be compared with those of Blake, but we never encounter passages in his work that approach Blake's expressionistic freedom of touch.[45]

[41] In *The Bibelot*, vol. XX, Dec. 1914, p. 411 (quoted by Raymond Lister, *Edward Calvert*, 1962, p. 19).

[42] Russell, 33, ii.

[43] Binyon, *The Engraved Designs of William Blake*, 1926, p. 64, suggests that the stippled plate *Mirth* (Russell 27, 2nd state, repr. Binyon op. cit. pl. 14) was a 'trial run' for the 'new, freer style' of Blake's late engravings; but it has none of the features that are conspicuously new in the *Job* series.

[44] The second edition of Thornton's *A Family Herbal: or Familiar Account of the Medical Properties of British and Foreign Plants . . .*, 1814, was 'illustrated by two hundred and fifty-eight engravings from plants drawn from nature by Henderson, and engraved by Bewick of Newcastle.' The drawings were sent up from London and Bewick's apprentices cut them generally in a straight-forward 'black-line' reproductive fashion.

[45] There is almost no common ground between the two artists. A block such as the vignette of *Fishermen by moonlight*, published in *A Memoir of Thomas Bewick written by Himself*, 1862, p. 184, might be cited as showing some technical similarities with Blake's woodcuts (in this case the bold rendering of the foreground); but this was a late engraving and very probably the uncertain work of an apprentice hand.

The essence of Bewick's style is that each stroke of the graver on the wood conforms to some clearly defined function in the statement of form or the establishment of texture or tone. Each mark is measured. It is an art of miniature, which Blake's emphatically is not.[46] Bewick's style derived, much more directly than Blake's, from engraving on copper, which had been brought to a point of great articulacy and discipline in the late eighteenth century by William Woollett[47] and his school. Bewick greatly admired Woollett; he copied his famous *Spanish Pointer*, after Stubbs, for the portrait of that dog in his *General History of Quadrupeds*,[48] and could write:

'I have often thought, had William Woolett been a Wood engraver, he would have shown its excellence long ago—his prints, from copper have not been equalled, but from the nature of the wood & the effect it produces, he would have advanced a step farther & on it, have outdone his excellence on copper.'[49]

Bewick's engraving on wood is, in a sense, the logical extension of Woollett's on copper. Blake, on the other hand, thought Woollett 'etch'd very bad himself'; he associated him with the French-trained and rather old-fashioned engraver Sir Robert Strange,[50] and denounced them both as 'heavy lumps of Cunning & Ignorance, as their works shew . . . the Life's Labour of Ignorant Journeymen, Suited to the Purposes of Commerce no doubt, for Commerce cannot endure Individual Merit'[51]—Woollett, in fact, belonged to the same world of dead materialism as Thornton. But Blake 'knew the men [Woollett and Strange] intimately, from their Intimacy with Basire, my Master':[52] there was a direct connection between Blake's training as an engraver and the school of reproductive printmakers headed by Woollett. In the reproductive engravings that Blake made throughout his career, he drew on the technical resources of that school; indeed, the basic grammar of Woollett's technique is present even in such personal and Blakean plates as *War, or the Three Accusers*.[53] If they are more linear than Woollett, that is because their subjects are so:

[46] See Binyon, *Print Collectors' Quarterly*, 1917, p. 322: 'It is astonishing how much bigness and grandeur Blake contrived to get into these tiny prints, and yet leave us with no impression of being cramped.'

[47] William Woollett, 1735–1785.

[48] 1790, p. 324. The design is reversed in Bewick's print.

[49] Bewick, *Memoir*, ed. Iain Bain (Oxford, 1975), p. 194–5.

[50] Sir Robert Strange, 1721–1792.

[51] *Writings*, pp. 593–4.

[52] *Writings*, p. 593. James Basire's dates are 1730–1802.

[53] *The Separate Plates*, no. VII, pls. 12, 13.

Blake could suppress outline in his engravings when obliged to do so by his model; for instance, in the pair of plates that he executed after Watteau in 1782.[54] Even the print of the *Canterbury Pilgrims*, which was intended to 'redeem my country' from the 'Coxcomb situation'[55] created by Woollett, is reliant on much of the technical language that Woollett had made current. It is (quite the opposite of the case with the woodcuts) Blake's conception that makes for the profoundest differences.

The *Canterbury Pilgrims* represents a mid-point, as it were, between conventional 'Woollettian' engraving and the purely Blakean idiom that lives in the woodcuts and in the *Job* plates. It is a piece of what Blake conceived as 'public' art, couched in a quasi-classical format and dealing with a universal theme—it is 'a Complete Index of Human Characters as they appear Age after Age'[56] (we have already encountered one of these characters in the Plowman). The original painting is in Blake's 'public' medium of 'fresco' (tempera) and the print, at least in its earlier states, preserves something of the even tonality of that medium. Its surface is covered with hatchings of parallels, straight, rippling, or swirling, criss-crossed with line-and-dot and dot-and-lozenge devices, all of which can be found in *War*, and are traceable to the formulas of Basire and, ultimately, of Woollett. In the third state of the plate, further engraving and some burnishing has broken the even distribution of textures, and there is a stronger play of light and shade across the design. In particular the background becomes strangely sombre under the rays of a fitful dawn that seems to be a kind of easterly Aurora Borealis. The effect is to plunge the background into brooding mystery. That background is an extensive landscape—the most extensive ever drawn by Blake, though paralleled in scale, but not in size, by the panorama of the river in the drawing for block No. 16 of the *Virgil* set. He described it as 'an eastward view of the Country from the Tabarde Inn in Southwark as it may be supposed to have appeared in Chaucer's time, interspersed with Cottages and Villages'.[57] It consists, in fact, of low, undulating hills dotted with buildings—distant spires, barns and a thatched cottage beside a clump of trees—and figures showing white against the dark land. But for the absence of a flock of sheep it is the landscape

[54] *The Separate Plates*, nos. XXIII and XXIV, pl. 39.
[55] *Writings*, p. 593.
[56] *Writings*, p. 591.
[57] *Writings*, p. 588.

5. A rough proof taken by Blake from one of the blocks before the division and cutting down of the individual subjects. Original size. *Department of Prints and Drawings, British Museum.*

6. A rough proof taken by Blake from one of the blocks before the division and cutting down of the individual subjects. Original size. *Department of Prints and Drawings, British Museum.*

ILLUSTRATIONS OF IMITATION OF
ECLOGUE I.

First Comparison.

Second Comparison.

Third Comparison.

7. The three blocks cut by one of the trade engravers after Blake's original drawings.

To face page 10.

ILLUSTRATIONS OF ECLOGUE I.

lines 62, 63,

63, 64,

65, 66, 67,

68, 69, 70, 71, 72, 73, 74, 75, 76, 77, 78, 79.

8. The four engravings by another hand which illustrate Eclogue I and which immediately precede Blake's work for Philips's 'Imitation'.

of the woodcuts, and its lighting anticipates their half-day, half-night of innocence and experience. In blocks 8 and 9, for instance, we find the lattice-windowed cottage, and the spire of a village church gleaming beneath the distant hill. Blake makes no attempt, as do the other illustrators of the *Virgil*, to present a specifically Classical landscape. If anything, he shows an idealised medieval, 'Chaucerian' one; his figures, on the other hand, wear contemporary or simply Blakean dress according to their functions.[58] It is only in representing the seat of Menalcas and the house with the well-rolled drive (Nos. 10, 13) that he suggests Classicism, and that is the Neo-classicism of contemporary architecture—a modern, not an antique note. The only location that is pinpointed (by both Philips and Blake) is the predominantly 'medieval' one of Cambridge: in block 11 Colinet rests by 'distant Cam' and the Gothic pinnacles of King's College Chapel glitter under the moon in a scene of dim chiaroscuro that recalls Elsheimer's nocturnal landscapes.

It would no doubt have disgusted Blake to hear 'that infernal machine called Chiaro Oscuro'[59] invoked in connection with his work; but his use of it must be examined if we are to understand the effect he achieves in the *Virgil* blocks. He was perhaps hostile more to 'painterliness' than to chiaroscuro as such—he attacked the 'unorganised Blots & Blurs'[60] of artists such as Titian and Correggio, whom he classed with Woollett and Strange as 'Ignorant Journeymen'. But his complaint that 'Every Picture has the same Effect, a Piece of Machinery of Points of Light to be put into a dark hole'[61] might be thought to come close to a description of the dramatic lighting in his own woodcuts. It is worth noting, however, that while his contempt for painting not based on 'Outline' applies consistently to Correggio, the Venetians, Rubens, Rembrandt and Reynolds, in the field of engraving he reserves his venom for the modern school—that is, for those men who had increased the capacity of engraving to reproduce 'painterly' pictures. The traditional discipline of the graver

---

[58] If we read the tunics of Colinet and the 'untoward lads' as smocks (compare them with the 'jovial hinds' in block 17), all the characters wear generalised contemporary dress, except Thenot, who is presented as a Blakean philosopher in long robes without a period connotation (though with Biblical overtones). Compare the 'medieval' landscape of the woodcuts with that in the background of two of the *Job* engravings (Russell, no. 33, ii and v) where large Gothic churches are to be seen. Elsewhere, the *Job* landscape is 'patriarchal' with large classical or pre-classical ruins.

[59] *Writings*, p. 582.

[60] *Writings*, p. 596.

[61] *Writings*, p. 599.

had ensured that until modern times any subject, when engraved, was founded on the requisite substructure of draughtsmanship. The rich and subtle effects of light and shade in, say, Durer's *St. Jerome in his Study*[62] are achieved within a wholly legitimate line-engraving technique. The shifting lights and shadows of Blake's early engravings of *Job* and *Ezekiel*[63] seem to owe much to this model, and they anticipate the effect of the heavily worked final state of the *Canterbury Pilgrims* which I have already discussed. In his woodcuts, Durer did not point the way to any more atmospheric treatment of light, limiting himself to a purely linear mode; it was only in the chiaroscuro woodcuts of the Italians and such Northerners as Lucas Cranach that a broader conception of lighting began to develop; and here there was little concern for expressive, as opposed to decorative, use of tone.[64] A possible exception to this generalisation is Urs Graf, whose white-on-black prints (derived from the effect of drawings in white bodycolour on a dark prepared ground by him and artists such as Altdorfer) do exploit the dramatic highlighting of form in a predominantly black space. A print such as Urs Graf's *Satyr Family*[65] uses the wood block in a way that comes closer to Blake's technique than any other, anticipating the effect of such plates as the frontispiece to *America* of 1793. But on the whole, as in his own *oeuvre* so in the previous history of the print, we must look among engravings rather than woodcuts for precursors of the *Virgil* blocks. The suggestion of Elsheimer in the block of Cambridge just referred to points to the work of the seventeenth-century Dutch engraver of Elsheimer's subjects, Count Hendrik Goudt,[66] where we encounter a blend of vigorous linear engraving with rich chiaroscuro which provides just the kind of sympathetic precedent that might have acted on Blake's imagination. Goudt's print after Elsheimer's *Flight into Egypt*[67] is a large, very dark plate in which the salient forms are picked out with silver contours very much as the subjects emerge from darkness in Blake's woodcuts. A more elaborate example, with large-scale figures and a wealth of linear detail treated

[62] Meder no. 59.

[63] *The Separate Plates*, nos. III and VIII, pls. 6, 7, 15.

[64] Binyon (*Print Collectors' Quarterly*, 1917, p. 322) points out the use of white line by such Italians as Giuseppe Scolari. Scolari's manner, however, is closely allied to the 'painterly' techniques of the Venetian school, and he often exploits the white line to suggest the swirl of brush-strokes—an effect very much at odds with Blake's conception of the engraving.

[65] Koegler no. 174; repr. Emil Major and Erwin Gradmann, *Urs Graf*, Basel, n.d., pl. 125.

[66] See Henry Scipio Reitlinger, 'Hendrik, Count Goudt', *Print Collectors' Quarterly*, vol. VIII, 1918, pp. 231–245. The name of Elsheimer was mentioned in connection with Palmer and the Ancients by Raymond Lister, *British Romantic Art*, 1973, p. 173.

[67] Dutuit no. 3.

in this way, is the *Mocking of Ceres*,[68] which was copied by Hollar in 1646;[69] and the best-known of all the Elsheimer subjects, *Jupiter and Hermes in the House of Philemon and Baucis*,[70] may well have been consciously or unconsciously in Blake's mind when he made his own design of Thenot and Colinet at supper, block 15. Prints by Goudt, or Jan van de Velde[71] whose night-pieces resemble his—the *Vesper* and *Nox* from the *Four Times of the Day*[72] for instance—are likely to have been among the many engravings in Blake's sadly undocumented collection, and will have interested him, if at no higher level, at least as examples of boldly inventive engraving technique. The development of the medium further in this direction was effectively halted by the invention of mezzotint, which was specifically adapted to interpret the sort of painting that Blake most despised, and was essentially a tonal and not a linear medium. Blake saw his own art as an engraver as a revival of the virtues that were submerged or perverted by the rise of the mezzotint. We should therefore look at the *Virgil* woodcuts as designs conceived in terms of the incised line; this adds a fresh dimension to their achievement as essays in chiaroscuro. It explains, too, the oddly prosaic nature of the preparatory drawings, which state the subjects in line alone, but line that needs to be realised by the graver, with its special, incisive, life-giving strength—a vital tool in Blake's expressive workshop.

The twenty drawings[73] that he made for the woodcuts are in pencil, with a little brown wash added with pen or brush to strengthen them. There is almost nothing in them to suggest the power and intensity of the final blocks.[74] But they show us, in their simplicity, how literally Blake follows Philips in every detail. I have already remarked on his inclusion of King's College Chapel in response to Philips's reference to

---

[68] Dutuit no. 6.

[69] Parthey no. 273.

[70] Dutuit no. 5.

[71] See William Aspenwell Bradley, 'The van de Veldes', *Print Collectors' Quarterly*, vol. VII, 1917, pp. 64–76.

[72] Le Blanc, vol. IV, 119–120.

[73] The drawings include one design for an unused subject, *Thenot and Colinet with their Flocks*; there is no study for the frontispiece. The whole group were in a sketchbook in the Linnell collection, sold at Christie's, 15 March 1918, lot 205. It was sold again in New York by the American Art Association, 22 April 1924, lot 60, and then split up. The drawings are now in several private collections. See the Nonesuch edition of the Woodcuts, 1937, p. 16, and *The Pencil Drawings of William Blake*, ed. Geoffrey Keynes, Nonesuch Press, 1927, where sixteen of the pencil designs are reproduced (pls. 50–54), including the three 'comparisons' of which we do not have Blake's own blocks.

[74] Herbert Furst, 'The Modern Woodcut', *Print Collectors' Quarterly*, vol. VIII, 1922, p. 165, says: 'one need only glance at them [the Virgil prints] to see that if they were not wood-engravings there would be no *raison d'etre* for the manner of their design.'

Cambridge (the poet had obtained his B.A. at St. John's College in 1696, and his M.A. there four years later). Even the images that seem to us quintessentially Blakean derive from the Imitation. The aerial figure that runs dancing along the horizon in block 4 is simply a vivid realisation of Philips's character of 'Lightfoot'; and the shining fruit that weigh down the branch of a tree in block 3 are also specified in the text, as is the eclipsed moon over a field of mildewed corn in block 6. To this extent, some of the central motifs of the artists most influenced by the woodcuts, Palmer and Calvert,[75]—motifs that they have helped us to think of as Blake's own—really owe their origin to Philips: the iconography of the 'Ancients' springs almost as much from a literary tradition of Pastoral as from any visual one.

But the literary images were taken out of their context. Samuel Palmer's fruit-laden trees are not necessarily a symbol of the human frame bent with years, and his moons are not eclipses but crescents which preside benignly over rich harvests. The lowering, fateful undertones that Blake so carefully matches in his illustrations are dismissed and the rural microcosm transformed into a rustic Paradise without alloy—the 'country of Beulah' described in the *Pilgrim's Progress*,[76] which Blake himself adopted in more complex guise as his 'realm of the Subconscious . . . the source of poetic inspiration and of dreams . . . intermediary between Eternity and Ulro (this world of Matter).'[77] Blake's 'Beulah' has in fact been summed up in terms directly reminiscent of the atmosphere of the *Virgil* designs: it is 'a place of night, lighted by the Moon of Love'[78]—there is a parallel between the ambiguity of their tenebrous pastoral calm and the uneasy, transitory sweetness of Beulah. Calvert, like Palmer, found the woodcuts 'humble enough and of force enough to move simple souls to tears', but chose to see them as naive statements: 'They are done as if by a child', he said; and added that 'several of them are careless and incorrect',[79] which Dr Thornton might well have taken as corroboration for his own reaction. It was in this sentimentalised version that the message of the woodcuts was passed on. Calvert and Palmer saw in

[75] Samuel Palmer, 1805–1881; Edward Calvert, 1799–1883.
[76] See Lister, *Calvert*, p. 19. Bunyan's description of Beulah (*Pilgrim's Progress*, with 29 watercolour paintings by William Blake, ed. G. B. Harrison, Limited Editions Club, 1941, p. 202) uses the language of the *Song of Solomon* (II, 11–13). The name 'Beulah', meaning 'married', occurs in Isaiah, LXII, 4.
[77] S. Foster Damon, *A Blake Dictionary*, U.K. edition, 1973, p. 42.
[78] Damon, *Dictionary*, loc. cit. See Blake's *Milton*, page 30, line 5, Writings, p. 518.
[79] Samuel Calvert, *Memoir of Edward Calvert*, 1893, p. 19.

them the single aspect that suited their own temperaments and purposes:

'I sat down with Mr Blake's Thornton's *Virgil* woodcuts before me,' Palmer wrote,[80] 'thinking to give to their merits my feeble testimony. I happened first to think of their sentiment. They are visions of little dells, and nooks, and corners of Paradise; models of the exquisitest pitch of intense poetry. I thought of their light and shade, and looking upon them I found no word to describe it. Intense depth, solemnity, and vivid brilliancy only coldly and partially describe them. There is in all such a mystic and dreamy glimmer as penetrates and kindles the inmost soul, and gives complete and unreserved delight, unlike the gaudy daylight of this world. They are like all that wonderful artist's works the drawing aside of the fleshly curtain, and the glimpse which all the most holy, studious saint and sages have enjoyed, of that rest which remaineth to the people of God. The figures of Mr Blake have that intense, soul-evidencing attitude and action, and that elastic, nervous spring which belongs to uncaged immortal spirits.'

As an extended and articulate response to Blake's woodcuts by a creative artist deeply influenced by them, Palmer's remarks are of great value. They show clearly the interpretation that he placed upon them, and hence the foundation on which his own art was built. Ironically, they reveal a somewhat cosy, self-indulgent complacency in natural beauty—a very nineteenth-century, religiose reaction towards an idealised past—that is at the opposite pole from the taut, broad-based and suffering consciousness that Blake makes us aware of even while charming us with the 'intense poetry' of his designs. If at first Palmer's vision was fresh enough, intense enough, to produce images of real value from this recipe, his philosophy could not withstand the gradual erosion of that intensity. The slow decline of his art into blunted and nostalgic repetition was therefore inevitable. Blake, on the other hand, made his most inspiring contribution to the vision of the new generation when he was himself in old age. For that reason the woodcuts are the most compelling demonstration in all his work of the enduring vigour and sanity of his genius.

---

[80] A. H. Palmer, ed., *The Life and Letters of Samuel Palmer*, new edition, 1972, pp. 15–16.

AMBROSE PHILIPS

Imitation of Virgil's First Eclogue

INTRODUCTION

PHILIPS, an admirable poet, has ably imitated this first Pastoral of Virgil, and designates himself under the character of a shepherd, in order that he might publicly declare his gratitude to his patron; for he had come up a lad from Scotland to England with very scanty means, was attacked in his writings by ill-natured critics, and envious poets, but found at length a Mecænas (Addison, a poet, and one of the authors in the Spectator) who stood forward as his friend, and brought him into public notice. Like Spencer he has preserved in his Pastorals many antiquated words, which though they are discarded from polite conversation, may naturally be supposed to have place amongst shepherds. The scholar may convert these Imitations, if the teacher chooses, into Latin Verse, following Virgil for his model. THENOT is the *happy*, and COLINET the unhappy *shepherd*.

The figures in the left hand margin identify the block engraved to
illustrate the adjacent line. The text is as presented by Thornton.

THENOT AND COLINET

THENOT

1   Is it not COLINET I lonesome see,
leaning with folded arms against the tree?—
Or is it age of late bedims my sight?—
'Tis COLINET, indeed, in woful plight.—
Thy cloudy look, why melting into tears,
unseemly, now the sky so bright appears?—
Why in this mournful manner art thou found,
unthankful lad, when all things smile around?—
Or hear'st not lark and linnet jointly sing,
their notes blithe-warbling to salute the springs?—

COLINET

Tho' blithe their notes, not so my wayward fate;
nor lark would sing, nor linnet, in my state.—
2   Each creature, THENOT, to his task is born;
as they to mirth and music, I to mourn.—
Waking at midnight, I my woes renew,
my tears oft mingling with the falling dew.—

THENOT

Small cause, I ween, has lusty youth to plain;
or who may then the weight of age sustain;
when every slackening nerve begins to fail,
and the load presseth as our days prevail?—
3   Yet though with years my body downward tend,
as trees beneath their fruit in autumn bend,
spite of my snowy head and icy veins,
my mind a cheerful temper still retains.—
And why should man, mishap what will, repine,
sour every sweet, and mix with tears his wine?—
But tell me then; it may relieve thy woe,
to let a friend thine inward ailment know.—

COLINET

Idly 'twill waste thee, THENOT, the whole day,
should'st thou give ear to all my grief can say.—
4   Thine ewes will wander; and the heedless lambs,
in loud complaints, require their absent dams.—

THENOT

See LIGHTFOOT; he shall tend them close: and I
'tween whiles, across the plain will glance mine eyes.—

COLINET

Where to begin I know not, where to end.—
Does there one smiling hour my youth attend?—
Though few my days, as well my follies show,
yet are those days all clouded o'er with wo:
no happy gleam of sunshine doth appear,
my low'ring sky and wint'ry months to cheer.—
5   My piteous plight in yonder naked tree,
which bears the thunder-scar too plain, I see:
quite destitute it stands of shelter kind,
the mark of storms, and sport of every wind:
the riven trunk feels not the approach of spring;
nor birds among the leafless branches sing:
no more, beneath thy shade, shall shepherds throng
with jocund tale, or pipe, or pleasing song.—
Ill-fated tree! and more ill-fated I!
from thee, from me, alike the shepherds fly.—

[33]

THENOT

Sure thou in hapless hour of time wast born,
when blightning mildews spoil the rising corn,
or blasting winds o'er blossom'd hedge-rows pass,
to kill the promis'd fruits, and scorch the grass;
or when the moon, by wizard charm'd, foreshows,
blood-stain'd in foul eclipse, impending woes.—
Untimely born, ill luck betides thee still.—

6

COLINET

And can there, THENOT, be a greater ill?—

THENOT

Nor fox, nor wolf, nor rot among our sheep:
from these good shepherd's care his flock may keep
against ill luck, alas! all forecast fails;
nor toil by day, nor watch by night, avails.—

7

COLINET

Ah me, the while! ah me, the luckless day!
Ah luckless lad! befits me more to say.—
Unhappy hour! when fresh in youthful bud,
I left, Sabrina fair, thy silv'ry flood.—
Ah silly I! more silly than my sheep,
which on thy flow'ry banks I wont to keep.—
Sweet are thy banks; oh, when shall I once more
with ravish'd eyes review thine amell'd shore?—
When, in the crystal of thy waters, scan
each feature faded, and my colour wan?—
When shall I see my hut, the small abode
myself did raise and cover o'er with sod?—
Small though it be, a mean and humble cell,
yet is there room for peace and me to dwell.—

8

THENOT

And what enticement charm'd thee far away
from thy lov'd home, and led thy heart astray?—

COLINET

9   A fond desire strange lands and swains to know.—
Ah me! that ever I should covet wo.—
With wand'ring feet unblest, and fond of fame,
I sought I know not what besides a name.—

THENOT

Or, sooth to say, didst thou not hither rome
in search of gains more plenty than at home?—
10   A rolling stone is ever bare of moss;
and, to their cost, green years old proverbs cross.—

COLINET

11   Small need there was, in random search of gain,
to drive my pining flock athwart the plain
to distant Cam.—Fine gain at length, I trow,
to hoard up to myself such deal of wo!—
My sheep quite spent through travel and ill fare,
and like their keeper ragged grown and bare,
the damp cold green sward for my nightly bed,
and some slaunt willow's trunk to rest my head.—
Hard is to bear of pinching cold the pain;
and hard is want to the unpractis'd swain;
but neither want, nor pinching cold, is hard,
to blasting storms of calumny compar'd:
unkind as hail it falls; the pelting show'r
destroys the tender herb and budding flow'r.—

THENOT

Slander we shepherds count the vilest wrong:
and what wounds sorer than an evil tongue?—

COLINET

Untoward lads, the wanton imps of spite
make mock of all the ditties I endite.—
12   In vain, O COLINET, thy pipe, so shrill,
charms every vale, and gladdens every hill:
in vain thou seek'st the coverings of the grove,
in the cool shade to sing the pains of love:
sing what thou wilt, ill-nature will prevail;

and every elf hath skill enough to rail.—
But yet, though poor and artless be my vein,
MENALCAS seems to like my simple strain:
and while that he delighteth in my song,
which to the good MENALCAS doth belong,
nor night nor day shall my rude music cease;
I ask no more, so I MENALCAS please.—

THENOT

MENALCAS, lord of these fair fertile plains,
preserves the sheep, and o'er the shepherds reigns:
13   for him our yearly wakes and feasts we hold,
and choose the fairest firstlings from the fold;
he, good to all who good deserves, shall give
thy flock to feed, and thee at ease to live,
shall curb the malice of unbridled tongues,
and bounteously reward thy rural songs.—

COLINET

First then shall lightsome birds forget to fly,
the briny ocean turn to pastures dry,
and every rapid river cease to flow,
ere I unmindful of MENALCAS grow—

THENOT

14   This night thy care with me forget, and fold
thy flock with mine, to ward th' injurious cold.—
15   New milk, and clouted cream, mild cheese and curd,
with some remaining fruit of last year's hoard,
shall be our ev'ning fare; and, for the night,
sweet herbs and moss, which gentle sleep invite:
16   and now behold the sun's departing ray,
o'er yonder hill, the sign of ebbing day;
with songs the jovial hinds return from plow;
17   and unyok'd heifers, loitering homeward, low.